Ethel and Woof sat at the window.
"I wish we had snow," said Ethel.

After a while Ethel said,
“It has begun to snow.
I see snowflakes.”

The wind began to blow. The snow came harder and harder.

Ethel got her boots and coat. Then she got a pair of mittens and a hat.

Ethel and Woof ran in the snow. Ethel made tracks in the snow. "Follow me," said Ethel.

Then Ethel began to
throw snow at Woof.
Woof tried to bite
the snow.

Woof did not like the snow. It made his teeth hurt.

“Help me make a big snowman,” Ethel said to Woof. “I will show you how.”

Ethel went to the top of the hill. The snow came at Woof.

"Run, Woof," cried Ethel.

But the snow ran over Woof. Woof was in the middle of the snow.

Ethel began to dig
for Woof.
"You cannot be a
snowman, little fellow,"
said Ethel.

Soon Ethel had a big snowman. He had a hat and a bow tie. "But I have lost the pipe," said Ethel.

Ethel ran inside and came back with a box of marshmallows. "These are for us to eat," she said.

Woof dug in the snow.
He got the pipe.

“You are a cute little snowman,” said Ethel. “But the pipe is for the real snowman.”

Ethel and Woof sat in the snow.
"Marshmallows are good to eat," said Ethel.